TOPICS FOR DISCUSSION AND LANGUAGE PRACTICE

BOOK TWO

Mike Carrier, M.A.
and
Philip Sauvain, M.A.

HULTON EDUCATIONAL PUBLICATIONS

© 1980 Exercises: Mike Carrier

© 1976 Story sequences: Philip Sauvain

Illustrations: Ingram Wilcox

ISBN 0 7175 0856 0

First published 1980 by Hulton Educational Publications Ltd., Raans Road, Amersham, Bucks.

Printed by Interprint, Malta.
Photoset by Tring Photoset Ltd., England.

Contents

Notes for the teacher

Units

Discussion phrases

Notes to the teacher

This book, with its companion volume, aims to provide stimulating material for language development and discussion practice for the EFL student around the intermediate level. The two books are different in level:

Book 1 – Low intermediate to intermediate level
Book 2 – Intermediate to upper intermediate level

Course objectives

Through working with this course, the student should be able to:

a understand the main points of view in a given presentation
b summarise and present these points of view in a logical way
c express a personal point of view, and explain it
d take part in a group or class discussion using idiomatic language
e express disagreement with other points of view
f re-state the views of others (ie the characters in the visual stimuli) and discuss a continuation of the situations presented in the book.

Language skills

While working through the material in the book, the student will develop and practise several language skills, such as:

a reading for information, and for comprehension
b expansion and active use of vocabulary related to each topic
c oral practice of language functions such as agreeing, disagreeing, summarising points of view
d role-playing and discussion skills
e writing skills.

Organisation of the course

There are 28 units, each two pages in length. They can be studied in any order, as there is no grading between them. There is some thematic continuity between certain units, but this does not have to be adhered to. The teacher is free to select the units on the basis of the interest value of any topic or group of topics to his particular students. Units 1–18 follow the pattern below. Units 19–28, however, are more advanced and do not contain language work.

a **Visual stimulus** – the cartoon-style texts present the topic and situation of the unit
b **Vocabulary** – explanations of some of the words that may cause difficulty
c **Comprehension** – questions on the text
d **Language work** – intensive practice of one or more language points which occur in the text
e **Points of view** – questions and notes that will lead the students to re-state and summarise the points of view represented by the different characters in the text

f **What do you think?** – questions designed to elicit the students' own opinion about the text or wider topics. They are designed to be starting points for further discussion in class or in groups

g **Role-playing** – directions to students to help them re-use the language of the unit by taking the roles of the characters involved or acting out a situation that is transferable to their own experience

h **Written work** – suggestions for written activities such as letters, summary, composition or dialogue, which are based on or follow from the topic of the unit.

Method

The visuals of the left-hand pages should be seen as **Presentation** material, in conjunction with the **Vocabulary** notes. The **Comprehension** section and the **Language work** aim to give the students an opportunity to re-use the language of the unit, and practise it in detail. Both sections can thus be supplemented by the teacher's own questions or exercises, in situations where students need further practice.

The **Points of view** section should be used to give the students practice in summarising the views of other people, before they come to express their own opinions. In some cases, students are asked to speculate as to what the points of view of characters may be. This is to give them an element of transition between talking about known ideas and generating their own.

The questions in the **What do you think?** sections should not be dealt with until students are familiar with the language and topics of the unit. Otherwise students are likely to have difficulty in expressing their own ideas, due to lack of understanding of either the language or the information.

Role-playing is designed to give students opportunity to produce language in a more realistic way, with less control and guidance from the teacher. This can also be organised in groups, thus giving more students than usual a chance to speak in the short time available in a lesson.

The suggestions for **Written work** can be adapted or supplemented by the teacher to the needs of the particular groups of students, some of whom may not need any written follow-up work at all. Most of the suggestions entail the writing of letters or reports of fact rather than discursive essays, which are too complex for most students at this level.

Since the aim of this book is to stimulate discussion *between students* on the given topics, it is important that students are adequately prepared with vocabulary and ideas. It is therefore recommended that wherever possible the sections **Points of view, What do you think** and **Role-playing** are prepared by students in groups before being discussed/acted out in the full class. This reduces students' initial inhibitions, consolidates their language practice through inter-student talk, and gives the teacher more opportunity to circulate and monitor individual students. Each group should then have a 'secretary' to report back to the class as a whole. Through the different activities several students will have a chance to act as group secretary.

UNDER STRESS

Jean Schofield is 42 and lives with her husband and 3 children in a council house in a new town.

Jean works in a supermarket 5½ days a week.

Her husband Jack is an unemployed painter.

You don't go out to look for jobs — you just sit around all day expecting jobs to come from nowhere — they don't advertise in racing papers, you know!

Oh shut up! I've done my share — let them find me a job for a change!

If you think I like housekeeping and bringing up children and working full-time just to keep you in a chair all day you're wrong.

THAT EVENING:

We'll probably have to prosecute — your son was with them when they broke in...

Keith wouldn't be in trouble like this if you'd been a father to him.

Worse was to come:

What is it, Jack?

The TV company. They say unless we pay the rental we owe, they'll...

AT THE SUPERMARKET:

This is the second time this week - that's my last warning!

I won't be late again.

But Jean was late again. The twins were ill and Jack refused to help. When she got to work the Manager was waiting...

Right - you're fired!

Unit 1   Under stress

Vocabulary

council house – a house owned by the local council, cheap to rent

painter – a man who paints houses (not pictures)

I've done my share – I've done enough work in my life

to keep you – to pay for your food, clothes, etc.

to prosecute – to start legal action against someone in a court of law

broke in – forced their way into a house and tried to steal something

rental – weekly/monthly money paid to hire a television set

you're fired – you're not working here any more/you have lost your job

Comprehension

1 Where does Jean work?
2 Why did she lose her job?
3 What does Jack do all day?
4 What sort of newspaper does he read?
5 What has Keith done wrong?
6 What will happen if Jack does not pay the TV rental?

Language work

Look at this sentence from the text:
Let them find me a job for a change!
This sentence tells you that Jack's attitude is 'I don't care, it's not my problem.'
Now finish these sentences, using a phrase like the one above:

1 I'm sick of cooking for my husband . . .
2 I'm not paying the TV rental . . .
3 I don't care what the police do to Keith . . .
4 I didn't really like the job at the super-market . . .

Points of view

1 What does Jean think of her husband? What would she like him to do?

2 What could be the real reasons behind their son's problem? Why does he try to steal things?
3 What are the manager's reasons for firing Jean?
4 Why are Jean and Jack unhappy about the letter from the TV company? Why is this bad news for them?

What do you think?

1 What sort of life can this family expect in the future?
2 How could they make their life better?
3 Was the manager fair in telling Jean she had lost her job? Would you have done the same?
4 There are many people like the Schofield family. How do you think their troubles are caused? Are they to blame for their hard life, or is it society's fault?
5 Worrying about money, jobs and children can cause a lot of stress and tension. What effects can this have on people? What does stress do to you?

Role-playing

1 Imagine you are Jack, and you want to find out from Keith what he did with his friends when he broke into a house. Work out the conversation.
2 Imagine you are Jean, who is very unhappy and has decided to leave Jack and start a new life somewhere else. Act out the conversation they would have.

Written work

1 Write the official letter that the manager would send Jean, telling her that she has been fired.
2 Jack is applying for a job. Write the letter for him.
3 The local newspaper is reporting the court case in which Keith appeared. Write a report of the crime and the trial.

IT'S ALL IN THE MIND

Jill Hardy is a member of the Samaritans, an organisation set up to help people with their problems, particularly people who are thinking of committing suicide.

In Jill's town, if people want to get in touch with Samaritans, they ring 5000.

Hello, I saw your number in the paper.

I - I'm really desperate - I don't suppose you can help me anyway....

But...well...I thought I'd ring you just in case.

Jill let the caller talk. As a Samaritan she had to be a good listener. She tried to help people by getting them to tell themselves what to do.

I really am desperate.....

I emptied a whole bottle of tablets, but then I thought better of it.....

I'm better off dead, really.

I'm going to have a baby and I've no one to turn to.

I suppose I could have an abortion - but I haven't got any money and I don't know how to go about it anyway...

I'd sooner have the baby, I think.

Unit 2 It's all in the mind

Vocabulary

commit
  suicide   – kill yourself
get in touch
  with   – contact (e.g., by telephone)
desperate   – without hope
just in case   – in the hope that you might
                help me
I thought
  better of it – I decided not to do it
I've no-one to
  turn to   – I've no-one to ask for help
abortion   – an operation to get rid of an
                unborn baby
sooner   – rather/prefer to

Comprehension

1 What are the Samaritans? What do they do?
2 Who telephones the Samaritans? Why do they do this?
3 What did Jill do? Did she give her own opinions?
4 What was this girl's problem? What did she want to do?
5 What did she decide to do in the end?

Language work

Look at this sentence from the text:
I thought I'd ring you.
This is an indirect way of reporting what the girl thought – 'I think I will ring the Samaritans.' When we report things that we say or think or dream, we put the sentence in the past. Now do the same with these sentences, starting with the words given:

1 I have a villa in Cannes. (I dreamed . . .)
2 I am late for my meeting. (I thought . . .)
3 She plays tennis very well. (I said that . . .)
4 They are very rude to us. (We felt that . . .)
5 He sings very well. (I thought . . .)

Points of view

1 Why did the girl want to kill herself? Only because she was expecting a baby? What other reasons might there be?
2 Why did she then change her mind? What do you think she wanted to live for?
3 The girl telephoned the Samaritans for help – what sort of help was she expecting?
4 She said she had no-one to turn to – why didn't she talk to the father of the baby? Why couldn't he help her, do you think?

What do you think?

1 The Samaritans receive a lot of telephone calls from unhappy people. Why don't these people talk to their family or friends? What does this tell you about the society they live in?
2 Why do the Samaritans only listen to problems, and not try to give advice? What are the dangers here?
3 Do you think this girl's problem is a common one? What could other people do to help?
4 Why do people think of suicide when they are unhappy? What do you think stops some people from actually doing it?

Role-playing

1 Imagine you are Jill, and go on talking to this girl, starting at the point where the text finishes.
2 Imagine the conversation that took place when this girl told her boy friend that she was having a baby. Act out what they said to each other.

Written work

1 Many magazines have 'problem pages' where you can write for help and advice. Imagine you are this girl and write a letter asking for advice.
2 Imagine you work for the magazine which receives the letter and write a reply to it.

IN PAIN

Did you remember to take an aspirin darling?

Yes!

Dr. Smith started his rounds at 10.30 in the morning with a headache.

She's out of danger now, Doctor, but we have to keep giving her pain-killing injections.

First Call Mrs. Grey

He quickly forgot his own troubles when he visited the local hospital. A patient of his had been injured in a car accident that morning.

Second Call Mrs. Redman

She's not stopped crying, Doctor, and she pulls her little knees up to her chest. She seems to get a spasm, then she's quiet, then another spasm.

Nothing to worry about, Mrs. Redman. Just give her this medicine.

To be honest, Miss Black, I can't find anything wrong. I'm sure the pains are real but they can be brought on by worry, you know.

Third Call Miss Black

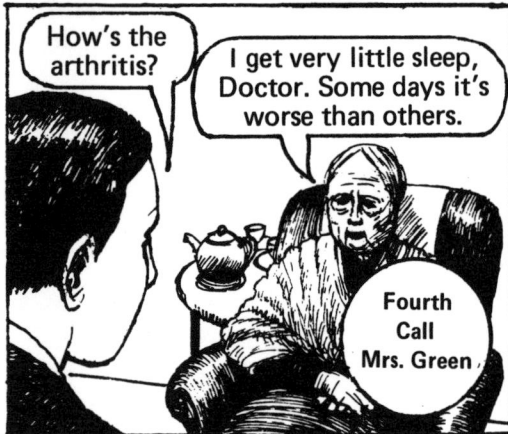

How's the arthritis?

I get very little sleep, Doctor. Some days it's worse than others.

Fourth Call Mrs. Green

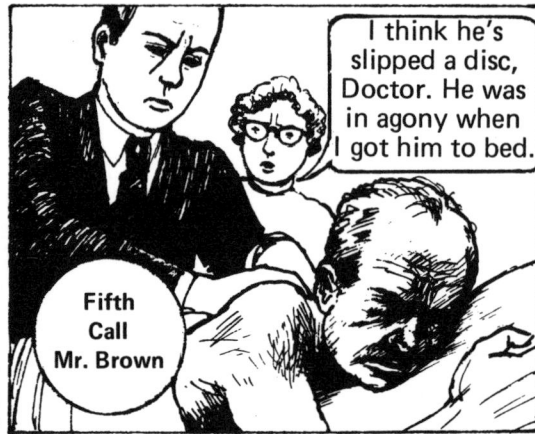

I think he's slipped a disc, Doctor. He was in agony when I got him to bed.

Fifth Call Mr. Brown

While he was at the Browns' he got an urgent call from the surgery to go to Mrs White. She was in labour.

Take it easy! When you get the pain breathe in deeply — that's it....

Sixth Call Mrs. White

Mrs White however had a relatively easy labour and the baby was delivered quite quickly.

It was nearly 2.30 p.m. by the time Doctor Smith got back to his home for lunch. His headache had gone, but he was now very hungry indeed.

I've been treating pains all morning and now I've got hunger pangs!

Unit 3   In pain

Vocabulary

aspirin	– a drug you take to stop pain
rounds	– visits to the homes of patients
injection	– a way of putting drugs into people with a needle
patient	– a sick person who is getting medical treatment
spasm	– a contraction of the muscles
brought on	– caused
arthritis	– a disease in the joints between bones
slipped a disc	– an injury to the back
surgery	– a doctor's office where he sees patients.
in labour	– the time just before a baby is born

Comprehension

1 Why did Dr. Smith take an aspirin?
2 Where was he going in the morning?
3 What made him forget about his headache?
4 What did he think was the problem with Miss Black?
5 Why couldn't Mrs Green sleep?
6 How did the doctor feel at the end of the morning?

Language work

Look at this sentence from the text:
I've been treating pains all morning.
This sentence stresses *how long* something has been happening. Now re-write these sentences in the same way:

1 I have learned Spanish for ten years.
2 He's had problems with his neighbours for ages.
3 We have planned this exciting holiday for months.
4 He has looked forward to his new job since Christmas.

Points of view

1 Why did the doctor forget his headache when he saw his patients? Could their problems perhaps make him feel worse?
2 Why does he visit these people at home? Why don't they visit him at the surgery?
3 Miss Black's pain might be caused by worry. What could be the cause of her worry? Is worry usually serious enough to make you ill?
4 The patients call the doctor by his title 'Doctor' and not by his name. What does this show about their attitude to him?

What do you think?

1 Some people seem to enjoy being ill, or thinking they are ill. Why? What pleasure do they get from pretending to be ill? Do you think any of the people here are pretending?
2 The doctor here was working only from 10.30 a.m. to 2.30 p.m. on his rounds. What do you think he would normally do during the rest of the day? Has he done enough work already?
3 None of these patients had to pay for the doctor's visit – it is all part of Britain's free health service. Do you think this is a good idea, or should people pay directly each time they are ill?

Role-playing

1 Imagine you are the doctor. What would you say to Miss Black, who is worried about something? Work out the conversation.
2 Imagine the doctor has found out that one of his patients is not really ill, but only pretending. Act out the conversation with another student.

Written work

1 Imagine what the doctor did during the rest of the day and write about it.
2 Write a letter to someone in your family, describing an illness you have had, and what the doctor did for you.

BLIND PEOPLE

John Shaw has been blind from birth. He has never known what it is like to see. He doesn't know what a human being looks like. He doesn't even know what he himself looks like.

As a child he was well-cared for by his family.

When he was old enough he went to a special school for the blind.

There he learned how to read using Braille.

Can you feel the dots with your fingers, John?

o1	o4	O	·	
o2	o5	·	·	= A
o3	o6	·	·	

Braille is a system where groups of 6 raised dots represent the letters of the alphabet. Thus dot 1 by itself represents the letter A.

John Shaw eventually learned to read very rapidly. His fingers raced over the raised dots.

That's splendid, John!

John's teachers also made much use of tape recordings, records and radio programmes. John made good progress at school.

He learned to play the clarinet.

He also enjoyed chess and many other games.

John's parents were worried that when he left school he would find it difficult to get a job. Many people do find difficulties here, but John was lucky.

He got a job in a recording studio. His hearing was very good and he found his job absorbing.

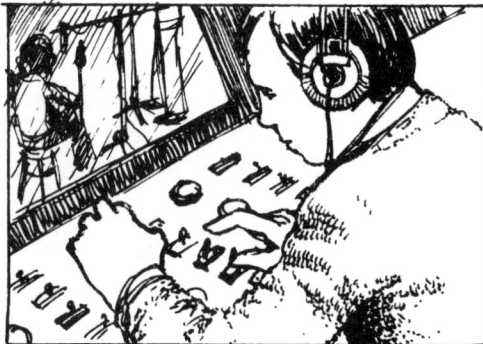

To enable him to get to work his parents managed to obtain for him a dog specially trained to lead him through the busy streets to the studio where he worked.

Unit 4   Blind people

Vocabulary

birth	– being born
cared for	– looked after
raised	– higher up
raced	– ran very quickly
dots	– points
eventually	– finally, in the end
absorbing	– very interesting
manage	– to succeed in doing something
enable	– make it possible for him
obtain	– get

Comprehension

1 When did John go blind?
2 How was he treated at home?
3 Where did he go to learn Braille?
4 What was he good at?
5 What sort of job did he get?
6 Why did he need a dog?

Language work

Look at this sentence from the text:
There he learned how to read using Braille.
Look at the way one word is in the 'to do' form and the next one is in the 'doing' form. Practise using these together by making full sentences from these groups of words:

1 He wanted/eat dinner/sit on the floor
2 I tried/play clarinet/stand on my head
3 He planned/go round the world/ride on a horse
4 She wanted/make money/sell antiques

Points of view

1 How does John feel about his problem? Does it prevent him from having a normal life?
2 What do you think John's parents felt when they found out their baby was blind? What difference would the dog make to John's life? What can he do that he couldn't do before?
3 Will the rest of John's life be the same as other people's? In what way might it be different in the future?

What do you think?

1 Do people in general give enough help to those like John who are blind? In what ways could we help them more?
2 Blind children go to special schools, and so only meet other blind children. Would it be better for them to be in normal schools and mix with the children there?
3 Some people are embarrassed by blindness and other handicaps, and try to avoid meeting anyone who is disabled in this way. What do you think is the cause of this prejudice?

Role-playing

1 Imagine you are John, going for an interview for a job at the studio. Work out the conversation with the employer with another student.
2 Imagine you are a reporter interviewing a famous blind person. Ask him or her how it feels to be blind. What do they believe the world is like?

Written work

1 Write a report about the help and training that blind people are given in your country.
2 Imagine you are blind, and write about the problems and the feelings you have during a normal day.

DEAF & BLIND

This is the true story of a remarkable woman. Her name was Helen Keller. She was born in 1880 in Alabama in the U.S.A.

When Helen was 1½ years old she contracted an illness which left her blind and deaf.

Her parents tried to do the best for their daughter and they employed a young teacher called Anne Sullivan. Anne herself had been almost blind in her youth.

Helen was a highly intelligent child. Frustrated by not being able to hear or talk, she often flew into tantrums.

w-a-t-e-r

Anne Sullivan persuaded Helen's parents to let her take her alone to a nearby house. After a fortnight of temper and tantrums, Helen quietened down. Anne began to teach her to spell.

Anne taught Helen to laugh....

...and often took her for walks in the country near her home.

Helen learned to write. Boards with lines on them helped her to keep the words straight.

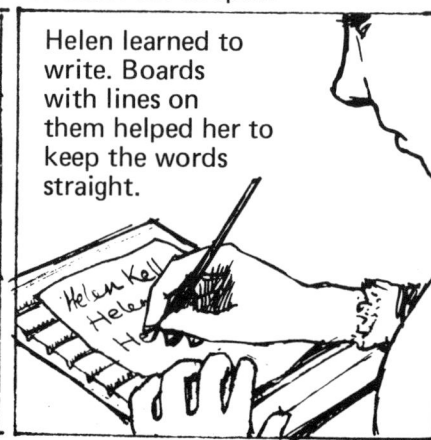

Later Helen was taught to speak. After ten lessons she surprised her teacher.

I am not dumb now.

Soon her talents were known all over the world. She was featured in newspaper and magazine articles. By the time she was 17 she was studying French, German, Latin, physics and many other subjects. She was still completely blind and completely deaf.

THE STORY of MY LIFE
HELEN KELLER

In 1902 she wrote a book which became well-known throughout the world.

Unit 5   Deaf and blind

Vocabulary

remarkable	– special, interesting
contracted	– caught (an illness)
youth	– the years when you are young
frustrated	– upset, discouraged because you cannot do what you want
quieten down	– become quiet
spell	– write (or say) the letters of a word correctly
tantrums	– fits of anger
dumb	– not able to talk

Comprehension

1 How did Helen become blind? What else happened at the same time?
2 Why did she often have tantrums?
3 Why was Anne such a good person to try to teach Helen?
4 What did Anne teach Helen to do?
5 Why did she need to use special boards to write on?

Language work

Look at this sentence from the text:
Frustrated by not being able to hear or talk, she . . .
This is a different way of saying:
She was not able to hear or talk. She was frustrated by this.
Now re-write these sentences in the same form as the example:

1 She was able to speak. She was surprised by this . . .
2 She was not able to find her mother. She was frightened by this . . .
3 I heard him say something rude. I was angry at this . . .
4 I saw my friend in the street. I was pleased at this . . .

Points of view

1 Why was Helen frustrated? How could she know what she was not able to do?

2 How did her parents feel when her illness happened? Why do you think they employed Anne to help?
3 Anne obviously worked very hard with Helen. What do you think was her main purpose? How would she feel when she heard Helen speak?
4 Why did Helen Keller become famous? What was special about her?

What do you think?

1 How is it possible for someone with no sight or hearing to learn what Helen learned? Could all deaf and dumb people do this, or was she a special case?
2 In what ways would her situation be different today, with modern medicine and technology?
3 How could Helen's example help other people throughout the world, not only those who are blind and deaf?
4 Helen became deaf and blind at the age of one and a half. Would the experience be different for someone who had this illness at the age of fifteen or forty-five? In what ways? Would it be easier or more difficult to accept?

Role-playing

1 You are a television interviewer talking to Helen about her life. Work out the conversation with another student.
2 You have some friends whose child has been born deaf and dumb. Imagine the conversation you would have, trying to make them feel better.

Written work

1 Imagine you have been blind since birth, but now you can see. Describe what you feel and what you find most interesting.
2 You are an architect designing a home for blind people. Describe all the features you would include to make life easier for them.

RETIREMENT

Patrick and Ruby Reilly have lived for 60 years in Belfast.

Pat has just retired after working in the shipbuilding yards for 32 years. Pat and Ruby have plans.

The solicitor says the completion date is August 19th.

We'd better fix a date for the removal then.

I'll be sorry in many ways - but just think of that sea air!

All day and every day...

The Reillys had made their dream a reality— they had retired to a small semi-detached bungalow in a small coastal town.

Although the Reillys enjoyed the sea, they felt lonely. They didn't know anyone and by the end of three months there were only a handful of people who even knew them by name. As yet they had no friends.

Do you think we ought to start going to the Senior Citizens Club? We might make some friends there.

Are you feeling any better, dear?

Early in December Ruby had a bad attack of 'flu. Patrick was very worried. His pension was not enough to buy special food for her.

Christmas was a very lonely time. Ruby was too weak to do anything special. They watched television almost all the time. It was very cold. The sea did not look inviting. Nobody visited them.

Early in January their old next-door neighbours invited them to spend a couple of days back in Belfast.

The Reillys got on the bus as if they were going for a treat.

Unit 6   Retirement

Vocabulary

Belfast	– the capital city of Northern Ireland
retire	– give up your job when you are old
yards	– the place where ships are built
solicitor	– lawyer
completion date	– the date when they will own their new house
removal	– moving to another house
senior citizen	– polite word for old people
flu	– short way of saying influenza
pension	– money paid to retired people
treat	– a special occasion you enjoy

Comprehension

1 What was Pat and Ruby's dream for their retirement?
2 Why did they want to leave Belfast?
3 What was their problem in their new home?
4 What was wrong at Christmas?
5 How did they feel about going back to Belfast for a few days?

Language work

Look at this sentence from the text:
Do you think we ought to start going to the Senior Citizen's Club?
The word *start* takes a 'doing' form after it. So do many other words, for example:

to like	to hate	to stop
to try	to prefer	to go

Now use these words, with a 'doing' form, to answer these questions:

1 What do you like doing in your spare time?
2 What are you going to do at the weekend?
3 My car won't go. What should I do?
4 Which do you prefer, listening to music or going out?
5 I really like going climbing – do you?

Points of view

1 This couple had planned for a long time to leave. What were they expecting from their new life?
2 Why were they disappointed? Was this their fault?
3 Why were they excited about going back? Did they think their previous life had been better?
4 This story is not complete. What are the different possible endings to it?

What do you think?

1 What are the problems that retirement causes for people like Pat and Ruby? Is it different for men and women?
2 Is retirement a good thing? Or should people be able to carry on working if they wish? What are the advantages of each idea?
3 How should the state help old people when they retire? What do they deserve in return for working all their lives?
4 In some societies old people are thought to be wise and important. In others they are thought to be a nuisance, because they are not useful any more. What do you think?

Role-playing

1 Imagine the conversation between Pat and Ruby and their old neighbours when they meet again. Act out their reunion.
2 Imagine yourselves in the same situation – you must decide whether to stay in the same town, or move to the sea when you retire. Discuss this with another student and make a decision.

Written work

1 What would you like to do when you retire? Write a description of your ideal of retirement.
2 Write about old people in your country. What does society think of them? What help do they receive?

LIVING ALONE

Alice Williams is 75. She lives alone in a council flat in a Welsh town. When her husband was alive he used to bring home a good wage as a miner. Now she lives on the retirement pension. Alice is quite happy. She likes knitting and watching television. She goes to bed early.

But she often regrets the fact that she had no children.

As time goes on she finds it more and more difficult to make ends meet.

One winter there were a lot of power-cuts. Alice never felt the cold so much. The dark scared her.

When she was ill she was glad she had good neighbours —but she didn't like being dependent.

I'll call again tomorrow morning Mrs. Williams. Don't you worry.

Thank goodness I'm still independent!

Next day the doctor arrived.

It's time you thought seriously about going into a home. You'd be well looked after. You'd have many friends, and when you were ill you'd have help always on hand.

Unit 7   Living alone

Vocabulary

wage   – the money you earn (when it is paid every week)

knitting   – using wool and needles to make clothes

regret   – be sorry about something

make ends
   meet   – spend your money carefully to buy what you need

power-cut   – when the electricity supply is switched off

independent   – preferring not to ask for help

a home   – (here) an old people's home, something like a hospital

Comprehension

1 Why does Alice live alone? Does she like it?
2 What are her hobbies or interests?
3 What is difficult for her? What does she worry about?
4 What does she think of her neighbours?
5 What worries her about the future?

Language work

Look at this sentence from the text:
You'd have many friends.
This is a way of persuading people, giving them good reasons for deciding something. The full form is 'You would have many friends.' Now make similar sentences to persuade a friend to go on holiday abroad, making sentences from the notes here. Use the same form as the examples in the text:

1 more sun/clean air
2 new types of food/strange drinks
3 different people/new language
4 good time/relaxed

Points of view

1 Alice regrets having no children – so why didn't she have any?

2 She is very independent. Why does she want to be like this?
3 What are the doctor's reasons for suggesting Alice should go and live in a home?
4 What do you think is the attitude of her neighbours? Do they mind helping her? Would they be happier if she lived in a home?

What do you think?

1 What are the special difficulties for people who live on their own?
2 Why do some people choose to live on their own, even when they are young. Would you like this, or would you prefer to live in a large group of people?
3 Alice was frightened by the power-cuts in winter. Why do you think these happened? Why was she frightened?
4 Many old people like Alice have difficulties with money because their pensions are small. Should the state give them more money? Or should they have worked harder?

Role-playing

1 Imagine the conversation between Alice and her family (brothers, niece, etc.) discussing whether she should go into a home or not.
2 Imagine you are a doctor trying to persuade an old person to move out of his own home into a special home. Act out the conversation, giving the advantages and disadvantages.

Written work

1 Imagine you are old, and write a description of your life, looking back on the good and bad things that have happened.
2 Imagine you have just moved into an old people's home – write a letter to your children telling them about it.

the Immigrants

Mohammed Khan, his wife and family of four live in a back street in a Yorkshire industrial town.

Mohammed works in a textile mill.

Earlier Mohammed had tried to get more highly-paid jobs but he was always unsuccessful. He thought it was the colour of his skin that led to his lack of success; but he was always told that it was his inability to speak English well.

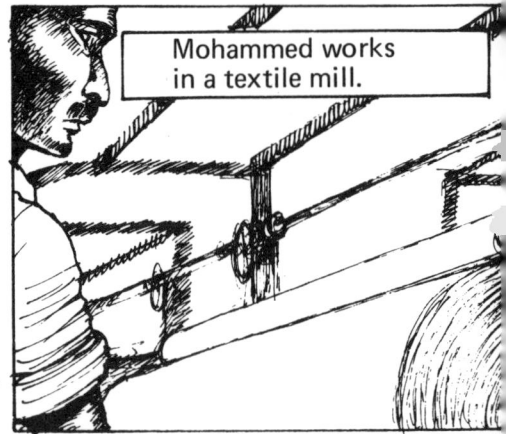

In the textile mill, he works long hours on the night shift.

Many other Pakistanis work in the same mill. Not surprisingly, his friends all live in the same district. They share customs, religion and language...

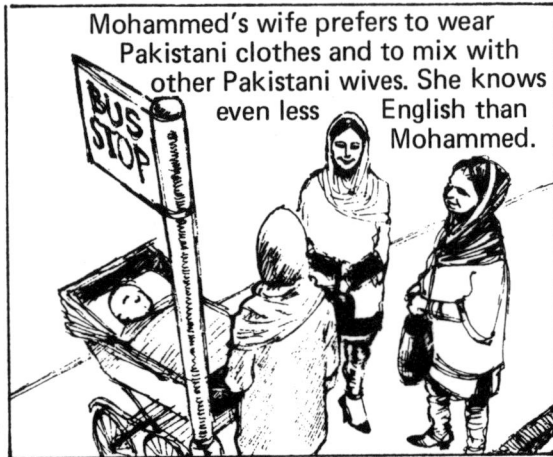

Mohammed's wife prefers to wear Pakistani clothes and to mix with other Pakistani wives. She knows even less English than Mohammed.

BUS STOP

With the children it is different, however.
They all go to school. Two go to comprehensive schools, and two to primary schools.

They speak English fluently and, like their friends at school, they speak it with a Yorkshire accent.

Hurry up — pass!

The children are bright and doing well at school. They are well-liked.

Like most children of their age, they enjoy television.

They are also keen football fans and often travel to Elland Road to support Leeds.

Unit 8 The immigrants

Vocabulary

textile mill	– factory for making cloth
led to	– caused
lack of success	– he didn't have any success
inability	– not being able to
shift	– a period of work, usually eight hours
fluently	– easily, with no hesitation
accent	– a special way of pronouncing
bright	– clever
keen	– very interested

Comprehension

1 Why is Mohammed unhappy in England?
2 Why can't he get a better job? What does he feel is the *real* reason?
3 Who are the people he works with in the mill?
4 What are the disadvantages of his job there?
5 Who are the people that he and his wife meet outside work? Whom do they meet socially?

Language work

Look at this sentence from the text:

Earlier Mohammed had tried to get more highly-paid jobs.

The *had* form shows that this happened before something else which has been described. It helps us to see what happened first. Now join these sentences together, using a *had* form to show which one happened first, and use the joining word shown in brackets:

1 The fire started. He arrived. (*before*)
2 The car exploded. It crashed. (*after*)
3 They were married for ten years. He left home. (*when*)
4 The man shot his brother. He had an argument with him. (*after*)

Points of view

1 Why do Mohammed and his wife prefer to be with other Pakistanis, and wear Pakistani clothes?
2 What does Mohammed feel the attitude of English people is towards him?
3 What is the difference between Mohammed and his children in their experience of England? What are the reasons for the difference?
4 Why do people like Mohammed decide to leave their home and go to another country? Is it a good idea? What special reasons do you think Mohammed had?

What do you think?

1 Many people are prejudiced against immigrants – they don't want foreigners in their country. Why do you think these unfriendly attitudes are common?
2 Not only Pakistanis but also Americans, Dutch people and many others come to live in Britain. Prejudice against them is not usually so strong. What reasons could there be for this?
3 What should individual people or states do to try to make life easier for immigrants and help them settle down? Should they control the number of immigrants who come into a country?
4 When Mohammed's children are older, they will not have the same problems with the language or customs of England. Does this mean there will be no prejudice against them?

Role-playing

1 Imagine you are Mohammed, going for an interview for a job. Act out the conversation with the English employer.
2 Imagine you are discussing the problems of immigrants with an English person, who is prejudiced. Work out the conversation with another student.

Written work

1 Write a letter to your family, imagining you are an immigrant, and explain the good and bad things you have found.
2 Write a description of what happens to immigrants who come to your country.

IN THE SLUMS

This is a slum in a town in the Black Country.

Ten people use this living-room.

Ralph and Edith Johnson, their seven children and Edith's mother live here.

Ralph is lazy, works occasionally and drinks.

Edith and her mother go to bingo five days a week.

The seven children play in the streets.

The house is dirty...

The children are unwashed...

...and ill-fed.

Unit 9   In the slums

Vocabulary

slum — poor part of town, or houses in very bad condition

Black Country — the industrial area in central England

occasionally — sometimes, not very often

bingo — a popular game of numbers, with prizes

ill-fed — eating only poor food and not enough of it

Comprehension

1 What is the problem in this house? Why is it uncomfortable?
2 Which conditions are bad for the children?
3 Why doesn't Ralph work regularly?
4 Where does Edith go in the evenings?
5 Where does Ralph go when he's not working?

Language work

Look at this sentence from the text:
The children are unwashed and ill-fed.
This is an impersonal way of saying 'The parents have not washed or properly fed the children.' Make impersonal sentences using the forms *had been done* or *was done* and re-write this description:

In the slums I saw cars that someone had abandoned. Thieves had stolen the wheels and taken the seats out. Somebody had painted slogans on the walls of the houses, and covered the windows with wood. Children had broken the windows, because their parents had left them alone at home all day.

Points of view

1 What reasons might there be for the overcrowding in the house?

2 Why does Ralph not want to work? Do you think he is trained for a job?
3 Do you think Edith and Ralph care about their children? Why are the children dirty?
4 How do you think this family see their situation? Do they think it's a bad situation, or are they satisfied?

What do you think?

1 Is this possibly a wrong or biased picture of their life? Is it true that some people live in dirty houses and do not wash?
2 If it is true, how can people get like this? Is there any way that other people can help them?
3 There has always been poverty and poor people, even in industrial countries. Is it a fact of life, or can something be changed?
4 What will this street and this family (or its children) be like in the future? Will the future be better? How can we be sure?

Role-playing

1 Imagine you are a social worker, sent to help this family. Give them advice on how they could improve their life. What will they say to you?
2 The children sometimes miss going to school. Imagine the conversation between the headmaster and the father, who is asked to explain why he doesn't send his children to school.

Written work

1 Edith needs more money for the children and is writing a letter to the council for help. Write the letter for her.
2 Write a description of poverty in your country, and what is being done.

MALNUTRITION

This is the story of a nameless family who lived in Bangladesh.

There were six members of the family and the father grew rice on a small plot of land.

They were never rich, but they could always point to neighbours who were poorer.

But in 1970 there were terrible floods and the entire region in which they lived was devastated. Many people were drowned, crops and homes were destroyed. Now they had nothing.

Through assistance from charities, their own government and other world organisations they managed to survive, but they only just got enough to eat. The children were always hungry.

Then a civil war started in their country. People were killed. Soldiers destroyed homes. Food became even more scarce. The family was scared.

Eventually they decided to flee to the nearby country of India and they joined the long lines of refugees escaping over the border.

Unit 10   Malnutrition

Vocabulary

malnutrition – not having enough food, having poor food
plot of land – piece of land
point to – show
devastated – destroyed, badly damaged, ruined
crops – food growing in the ground – e.g., corn or potatoes
assistance – help, aid
charities – organisations giving help to poor or homeless people
scarce – not easy to get
flee – run away from danger

Comprehension

1 How does this family compare with its neighbours?
2 What was the main crop that they grew on their land?
3 What was the cause of this great devastation?
4 What did they personally lose at this time?
5 Who tried to help these families?

Language work

Look at this sentence from the text:
Through assistance from charities . . .
Assistance is the noun from *to assist*. Now find out the nouns that come from the words in brackets, and re-write the sentences:
1 The (arrive) of the train was delayed.
2 We were very sad when we heard of his (die).
3 The plane was very full, and it was an uncomfortable (fly).
4 This is very important – you must make a (decide).
5 There's no time left, there can be no (hesitate).

Points of view

1 How did the family feel about being poor? Were they unhappy – or happy that they were not as badly off as their neighbours?
2 What were the possible causes of the civil war in their country? What do people normally fight about?
3 Why did the family decide to flee to India with the other refugees?
4 What did the family hope to do in the future? What were they hoping to escape from in their own country?

What do you think?

1 Even before the floods, these people were very poor. Why is there so much poverty in such countries?
2 Why is there such a big difference in the standard of living here and in industrial countries?
3 Can poverty be tackled by individual governments, or is it a world problem?
4 Some of these problems are caused by natural catastrophes like floods. Can anything be done to prevent or control such catastrophes?

Role-playing

1 Imagine you are fleeing with this family, and work out the conversation you might have with the guards at the border. What will they ask you?
2 Imagine you are a reporter, interviewing the President of a poor country. What would you ask him about?

Written work

1 Write a description of the family's life after this story.
2 Give your opinions on how to fight poverty in the future.

Victim of Violence

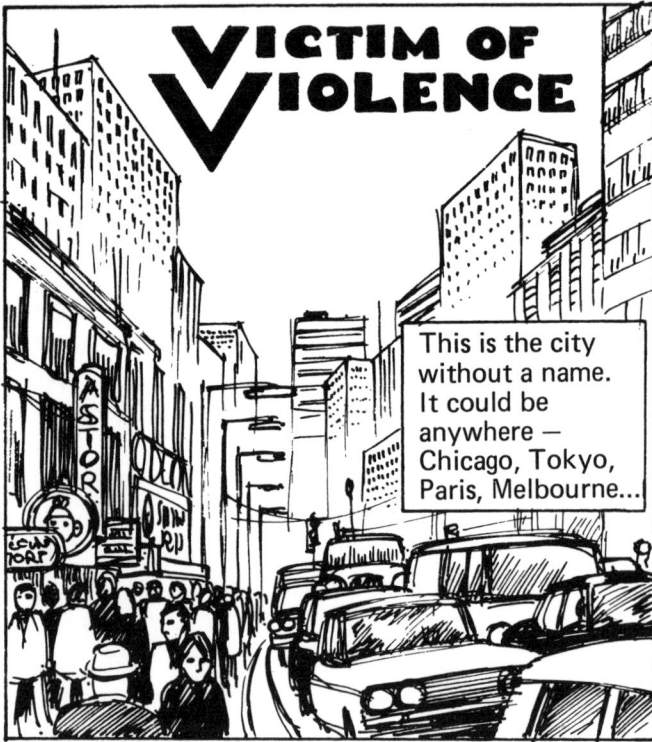

This is the city without a name. It could be anywhere — Chicago, Tokyo, Paris, Melbourne...

This is the story of a violent riot. It began peacefully enough with a demonstration - just a crowd of people with placards...

An extremist group in the crowd wanted to see some action. They looked round for a target.

The target was not hard to find. As is always the case, the police were there to see that the demonstration was peaceful.

Some of the police were a little too enthusiastic, but their officers managed to control the situation and kept the crowd in hand.

But there were fights; stones were thrown at the police.

The police used their batons and riot gas.

One innocent bystander —a child—was hit in the face by a flying stone.

Unit 11 Victim of violence

Vocabulary

victim   – person who is injured by someone else's action
placards   – posters, large signs
target   – a thing to aim for (usually: in shooting a gun)
in hand   – under control
batons   – long sticks used by the police
bystander – someone standing by, not taking part

Comprehension

1 Where is this demonstration happening?
2 Why are the police present at the demonstration?
3 How did some of the police act while trying to control the crowd?
4 Who caused the violence? Who was the violence aimed at?
5 What happened to the innocent bystander?

Language work

Look at these sentences from the text:
Stones were thrown at the police.
One innocent bystander – a child – was hit in the face.
These are more examples of the impersonal sentences discussed in Unit 9. We use them when we don't know who did the action. Use these forms to re-write this description. Make sure you leave out all the words you don't need (like 'someone') when it's an impersonal sentence.

Someone threw a stone at the policeman, who fell down bleeding. Someone carried him to an ambulance, which took him to hospital. There someone looked after him and gave him some painkillers. The doctors kept him in bed for a day and then allowed him to go home. His senior officer gave him a week off to rest.

Points of view

1 Why do the different groups want to demonstrate on the streets?
2 Why do the police think they must control crowds? What would happen if they were not there?
3 If the demonstrators want publicity for their ideas, why do they fight with the police?
4 What effect do these events have on the family or friends of the people injured? What is their attitude to demonstrations?

What do you think?

1 Is it a good idea for police to carry guns at demonstrations? Does it mean there will be less or more violence?
2 Demonstrations have become popular all over the world, but are they useful? What good or bad effects do they have?
3 What alternatives are there to noisy and violent demonstrations? In what other ways can society be changed?

Role-playing

1 Imagine the conversation between a demonstrator and the policeman who arrested him. What will they say to each other?
2 With two students, act out a television discussion between the Chief of Police and the student in charge of the demonstrators in a town.

Written work

1 Write a description of a demonstration you have seen or heard about as if you had actually been there.
2 Choose a political subject you are interested in and describe why a demonstration would be either a good or a bad idea.

VICTIMS OF WAR

These people live in an area between two countries which disagree about their border. For many years now they have been the victims of a long and cruel war. Time and time again they have had to flee their homes as the enemy advances.

Some people are too old to escape. They stay, hoping their lives and homes will be spared.

When the enemy advances, shells, bombs, napalm, bullets create chaos. Many civilians die.

These are the horrors of war.

When the enemy retreats, the same thing happens all over again.

This is just one among many areas of the world where civilians have been victims of war since 1945.

Unit 12   Victims of war

Vocabulary

border	– line between two countries, frontier
time and time again	– many times
spared	– saved, not attacked
napalm	– a chemical used in war which burns people's skin
retreat	– go back
civilians	– ordinary people, not soldiers

Comprehension

1 Why have these people had to leave their homes?
2 Why are the two countries fighting?
3 Why don't the old people try to escape?
4 What do the soldiers do when they advance?
5 How is this country similar to other parts of the world?

Language work

Look at this sentence from the text:
They stay, hoping their lives and homes will be spared.

This is a more interesting way of joining sentences than 'They stay and they hope'. Now join these sentences in the same way, using the *-ing* form:

1 The enemy advanced and killed many civilians on the way.
2 The government said they were winning and they knew it was not true.
3 The families fled over the border, and left all their things behind.
4 The soldiers stole the refugees' possessions and sold them in the city.

Points of view

1 What might be the reasons behind the border disagreement? Why is it so important where the border lies?
2 When soldiers are fighting each other, why do they kill civilians also? How does it help them win?
3 What – if anything – might the government do to help these people and protect them?

What do you think?

1 Wars can have many causes. What caused some of the major wars in the last hundred years?
2 Did these wars bring any advantages for ordinary people in the countries that started the wars?
3 Some people think that governments start wars not for political reasons, but for economic reasons. They can then build new factories, give jobs to everybody, etc. Do you think this is true?
4 Is war less popular now? Are there fewer wars today than there were before?

Role-playing

1 You are interviewing the Prime Minister of the country in the story. What will you ask him about the war, and what will he say?
2 Imagine you are talking to refugees from this war. What will they say about their own government and soldiers?

Written work

1 Write your opinions about war, giving reasons why it is necessary or unnecessary, as you prefer.
2 Find out about a famous war of the past, and describe how and why it happened, and who benefited from it.

RACING DRIVER

John Lewis, a Fleet Street journalist, and his girl friend were having a drink to celebrate John's return after covering the Le Mans event.

What was it really like, John?

Well, for me it started with the interviews.

I tried to get as much information as I could on how the drivers felt about Le Mans.

Many of them criticised the race...

Too many slow cars getting in the way of too many quick ones!

Too many regulations!

It's a matter of luck, not skill, if you finish.

But others looked forward to it

Great! The best test of man and motor in the world.

At 4.0 p.m. the cars approached the start line after the engines had been checked.

Then the track came alive with the roar from exhaust...

Two Matras quickly took the lead, followed by two Ferraris...

But within minutes there was trouble as one car crashed off the track and burst into flames.

Unit 13 Racing driver

Vocabulary

Fleet Street	– the street in London where newspapers are produced
celebrate	– have a drink/meal/party to show you are happy about something that has happened
cover the event	– report on what was happening
regulations	– rules
it's a matter of luck	– luck is the most important thing
roar	– loud sound (like an angry animal)
exhaust	– the pipe where fumes come out of a car
took the lead	– got in front of the other cars
burst into flames	– started to burn

Comprehension

1 Where had John been? Where is he now?
2 What had John done to find out about the race?
3 What did many drivers think about the organisation of the race?
4 When did the race start?
5 What happened immediately after the start?

Language work

Look at this sentence from the text:

John Lewis and his girl friend were having a drink to celebrate John's return after covering the Le Mans event.

After covering is a short way of saying *After he had just covered* the event. Now join these sentences together with *after* and use this short form:

1 He came home late. He had worked overtime.
2 He watched television. He had cooked his dinner.
3 He went to the cinema. He had washed the dishes.

4 He telephoned his brother. He had come home.
5 He went to bed. He had had a bath.

Points of view

1 Why did John's newspaper think it worth while to send him to France to watch a race?
2 Some drivers criticised the organisation, so why did they continue with the race and not leave?
3 Why are there so many cars so close together at the start of the race? Is it dangerous?
4 How do you think the crash was caused? Is this unusual in motor-racing?

What do you think?

1 Racing drivers are often killed. Why, then, do these men continue to take these risks? What is the attraction of racing?
2 Many drivers become very rich – is this the attraction of racing? Is it worth risking your life to become rich?
3 Why do people risk their lives on other dangerous sports like mountaineering or diving? Is danger exciting in itself?
4 Why do you think women don't often take part in dangerous sports? Is it because they don't have the opportunity?

Role-playing

1 Imagine you are a reporter finding out about the crash in the race at Le Mans. Make up your conversations with the drivers and the owner of the racetrack.
2 Act out the conversation between the driver of the car which crashed, and his wife. He is injured, and she is trying to persuade him to give up the sport.

Written work

1 Write a description of the accident from the point of view of the driver of the car.
2 Write your reasons for wanting to be a racing driver. Imagine you have become famous in the sport.

FIRST MEN ON THE MOON

Cape Kennedy, U.S.A.

On Wednesday 16th July 1969 Neil Armstrong, 'Buzz' Aldrin and Michael Collins set off on an incredible journey to the moon.

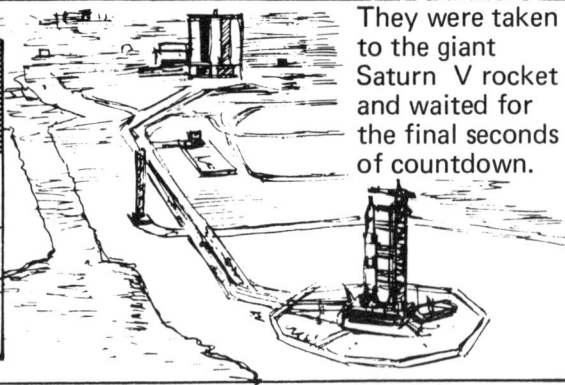

They were taken to the giant Saturn V rocket and waited for the final seconds of countdown.

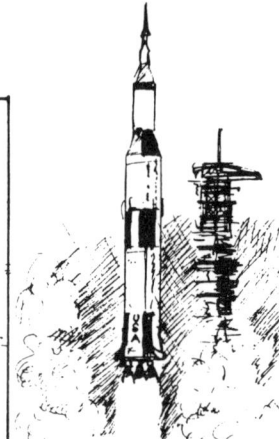

6-5-4-3-2-1-Zero !

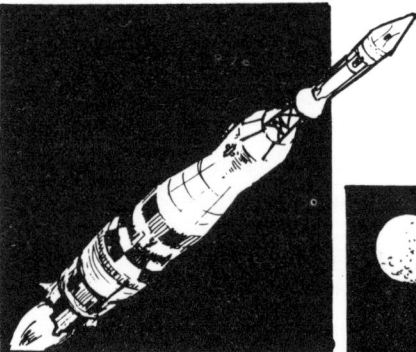

In less than 3 minutes the rocket was only $\frac{1}{3}$ its original weight.

Within $1\frac{1}{2}$ hours the crew fired the rocket motor which was to take the Apollo 11 spacecraft on course for the moon.

It's really a fantastic sight!

Three days later they were orbiting the moon.

Armstrong and Aldrin crawled into the lunar module 'Eagle'.

The two space vehicles separated.

As they neared the moon's surface Armstrong took control to avoid hitting a crater

At last the lunar module landed.

That's one small step for a man, one giant leap for mankind.

At 3.56 a.m. British time, Neil Armstrong stepped on to the surface of the moon.

Unit 14 First men on the moon

Vocabulary

Cape Kennedy – place in America where rockets are sent into space

incredible – hard to believe, amazing

Saturn V – the name of the rocket

countdown – the last seconds before the rocket goes off

crew – the people in the rocket who control it

Apollo 11 – the name of the spacecraft

orbiting – going round (the moon) in a circle

crawled – moved along on hands and knees

lunar module – the part of the spacecraft that would land on the moon

crater – big hole in the surface of the moon

leap – jump

Comprehension

1 How long did the journey take?
2 What did the rocket lose on the way?
3 What was the name of the special part that landed on the moon?
4 How many men landed on the moon? Who was the first to walk on the moon?

Language work

Look at this sentence from the text:

Armstrong took control to avoid hitting a crater.

Avoid is another word that takes *-ing* after it. So do the words: *suggest prevent* and *see*. Now re-write these sentences, putting in the *-ing* form where it is needed:

1 He agreed when I suggested (go) to the cinema.
2 He ran away to avoid (pay) for the books he had picked up.
3 She said she wanted to see me (dance) in the discotheque.
4 She did her best to prevent me (leave) my job.

Points of view

1 How did Armstrong and the others feel about travelling through space?
2 Why did the American government send them there? What advantages could there be?
3 What do you think Armstrong meant by a 'giant leap for mankind'? What might mankind learn from the moon trip?

What do you think?

1 Is it right to spend a lot of money on moon trips and other space journeys? Could the money be spent more usefully in other ways?
2 Should we send people to other planets as well as the moon? What might we find there?
3 Might there be life somewhere else in the universe? If so, what is the best way to make contact?
4 Many people believe they have seen flying saucers or UFO's – unidentified flying objects. Do you believe they exist? If so, why are they visiting us?
5 Should space travel be a sort of race between certain countries or should many nations share in it?

Role-playing

1 Work out an interview with Neil Armstrong, asking him about his walk on the moon.
2 Act out an argument between two scientists; one believes space travel is a waste of money, the other is very interested in finding out about other planets. Each should try to persuade the other.

Written work

1 Write a description of the moon landing from the point of view of Michael Collins who stayed circling in the spacecraft.
2 Write a fantasy story in which you meet people from another planet.

A COMMUNITY

John Archer lived with his wife Audrey and their two young children in a street in a large industrial city. His father and mother lived in a similar house two streets away. Audrey's widowed mother lived next door.

Having lived in Victoria Terrace all her life Audrey reckoned she knew everyone in the street very well.

She liked having her mother next door, too. She felt she could keep an eye on her that way.

John liked the friendly atmosphere and the pub on the corner, but he found not having a garage a nuisance.

When a crisis or problem occurred everyone helped to 'sort it out' but this was before the Council announced that the area was to be cleared.

They're going to re-house us in tower blocks of flats!

BREAK-UP OF A COMMUNITY

A journalist found out about the resentment in the district and his paper featured several stories on the subject.

But it was no use....

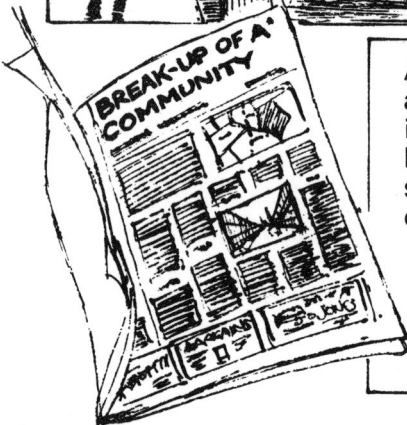

...One spring the people of Victoria Terrace and the streets nearby moved into the Carlton Towers.

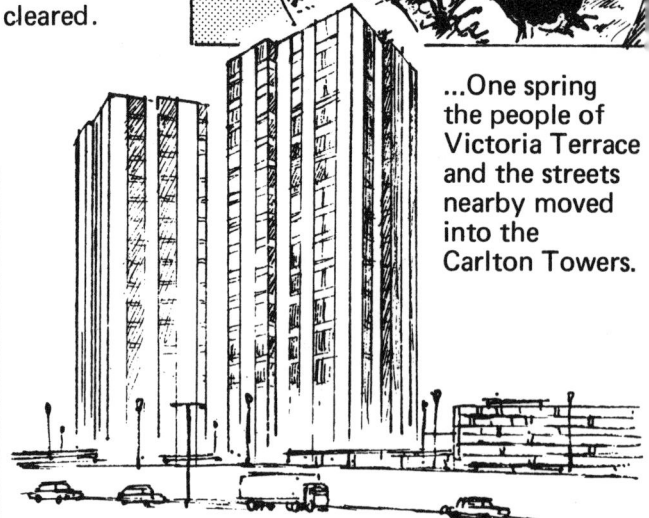

Unit 15 A community

Vocabulary

community   – a group of people who live or work together
terraced   – houses joined to each other in a long line
widowed   – describes a woman whose husband has died
reckoned   – colloquial for 'thought'
keep an eye on– look after, see that everything is all right
nuisance   – something annoying
occurred   – happened
tower block – tall thin apartment buildings ('skyscrapers')
resentment   – bitterness and dislike about something

Comprehension

1 How did Audrey know everyone in the street where she lived?
2 Why did she like her mother to live close to her?
3 What didn't John like about living here?
4 Why did all the people have to move out of their street?
5 How did they feel about this?

Language work

Look at this sentence from the text:
The council announced that the area was to be cleared.
This is a report of what somebody said. But what they actually said was *The area is to be cleared.* When we report something, we put it into the past tense. Now re-write these sentences, in the same way as the example:

1 'This building is going to be pulled down,' said the architect.
2 'The local people want to keep the building,' replied the councillor.
3 'They will have to pay for repairs,' announced the council.
4 'That is the job of the council,' stated the action group.

Points of view

1 What was the atmosphere in the community? When the people in the street had problems who helped them?
2 Why did the council want to move everyone out of the street into tower blocks? What would the benefits be?
3 What did the local people think they would lose by moving into towers? Do you think some of the people were glad to move?
4 What was the purpose of the news stories about this plan? Whose side was the newspaper on?

What do you think?

1 What are the differences in living in tower blocks, compared with small terraced houses? Which would most people prefer?
2 How is the positive atmosphere of a community created? Is it because the houses are small, or close together? Or because the people have lived here all their lives?
3 Why are tower blocks more popular with councils than small houses?
4 The journalist wanted to influence the council with his reports. Do you think newspapers do have this sort of influence? Can they make governments change their policies? Should newspapers have this power or not?

Role-playing

1 Imagine you are the journalist, and interview the town planner who wants to move the people. Find out his real reasons.
2 Act out the conversation in the pub between someone who wants to move, and someone who wants to stay.

Written work

1 Write a comparison of life in the two types of housing, as experienced by one of the families.
2 Describe the community that you live in.

RAILWAY CLOSURES

Mike O'Brien (19) and Rachel Hall (18) lived in a small town at the coast. They were students at the Technical College in a large town about 30 kilometres away. Each weekday they caught the diesel which left at 8.30 a.m.

It's a wonder this line makes any money.

There's only a busload of passengers on board.

In fact the line didn't make money at all. It made a large loss. For much of the day the station was deserted.

At a news conference British Rail officials dropped a bombshell — the line was to be closed.

If we charged travellers what it costs to keep this line open, they would quickly turn to other forms of transport.

Most of them have already done so anyway. We just don't get enough passengers on this service.

Unit 16   Railway closures

Vocabulary

diesel — type of train with a diesel engine (not electric)

it's a wonder — I'm surprised

on board — on the train

deserted — empty, no people there

bombshell — (figurative) sudden, surprising news (usually bad news)

Comprehension

1 Why do these students need to travel by train every day?
2 Why didn't the line make money?
3 Why can't the railway make it profitable by charging more money?
4 What has happened to the passengers who used the train before?
5 Why did British Rail hold a news conference about this?

Language work

Look at this sentence from the text:

If we charged travellers what it costs . . . they would quickly turn to other forms of transport.

If sentences always have a special form:

If this *happened,* then that *would happen*

Now re-write these sentences, using the correct forms:

1 If the railway (lose) money, the company (close) it.
2 If the railway (close), students (not be able) to go to college.
3 If there (be) no buses to the town, the students (need) to move house.
4 If the students (go) by bus, they (spend) too much time travelling.
5 If the government (give) some money to the railway, it (not have to) close down.

Points of view

1 Although not many people use this train, some regular passengers are sure to be affected. If there is no train how will it change their lives?
2 What other sorts of passenger will be affected? Will the closing of the line affect the railway workers also?
3 If the railway company saves money by closing the line where will that money be used? Will other trains become cheaper?

What do you think?

1 Why isn't British Rail or the government prepared to keep trains running when they are not full? Isn't it better to lose money but give a good service?
2 What are the other forms of transport that the British Rail official talks about? Are they as cheap or easy as the train? Can everybody use them?
3 Should public transport be organised so that it makes a profit, or should it be helped by money from the government?
4 What are the arguments for having more public transport instead of private cars? Which system do you think is better?
5 Will it be possible in the future for more people to have private cars? How might the supply of petrol change the situation?

Role-playing

1 Imagine you are the British Rail official at the news conference. Answer questions from reporters and explain British Rail policy.
2 Work out a discussion between local people and the government minister who wants to close more railway lines to save money.

Written work

1 Write a description of what you think transport will be like in the year 2100.
2 Write a history of the different types of transport that have been used by mankind.

THE AIRPORT

When the question of having an airport for the city was first raised the people in one small village didn't think much about it until...

It says one possible site for the new airport is near here.

Let me see that.

NEW AIRPORT: COMMITTEE SHORTLISTS

BARGAINS

It's scandalous. We must get an action committee together. They're not going to get away with this.

But what can we do?

STOP THE AIRPORT

'AIRPORT' ACTION GROUP

TONIGHT: Meeting in Village Hall

AIRPORT ACTION GROUP

SAVE OUR VILLAGE

If an airport is built here we'll have no peace...

There will be noise, risk of accidents, traffic problems, maybe new industries. Our peaceful village will be unrecognisable...

Unit 17   The airport

Vocabulary

raised	– (here) when the question was asked
site	– piece of land where something will be built
scandalous	– disgraceful, shocking
get away with something	– do something which you should not do and nobody stops you
un-recognisable	– looking completely different

Comprehension

1 Why didn't the villagers at first take much notice of the news about the airport?
2 How did they find out it would be in their village?
3 What did they think of this plan?
4 What did they decide to do immediately?
5 How did they try to get publicity?

Language work

Look at this sentence from the text:
They're not going to get away with this.
Here is another example of the meaning of a word (*get*) being changed by an added word (*away*). Now finish these sentences by finding out which of the words in the list below will fill the gaps:

1 Sally was unhappy because her marriage had broken . . . .
2 Why don't you come . . . and see us this evening?
3 He said he had a lot of money and a house in France, but I didn't believe him. I think he was making it . . . .
4 I'm very busy. Can I put . . . our meeting till next week?
5 We want to go . . . tonight. Can you look . . . the baby for us?
Choose from: *up, down, off, out, after, round, over, on*

Points of view

1 Why are the villagers unhappy about having an airport near them? What are they afraid of?
2 What qualities must an airport site have?
3 If there was no need for an airport before, what reasons might there be for having one now? How can it be justified?
4 What do the villagers hope will happen after their public meeting? How do they hope to change the government's plans?

What do you think?

1 Is it realistic to try to stop the development of airports? Are there alternative ways of improving transport?
2 The villagers in the story want to protect their quiet lifestyle, but what else needs to be protected? What damage can a new airport cause?
3 Can you think of any advantages for an area where this sort of development takes place?
4 Is the development of new airports, roads, factories, towns, etc. justified if all we want is a higher standard of living? Should we sacrifice the countryside for such development?

Role-playing

1 Continue the public meeting in the story. Give the different opinions for and against the planned airport.
2 Plan, with other students, a campaign to persuade the government to change the plan. What will you do?

Written work

1 Write a report of the public meeting for the local newspaper.
2 Write a letter to your Member of Parliament, explaining why you are against the airport.

On Parole

You will serve three years in one of Her Majesty's prisons.

The prisoner's room was far removed from the common idea of a cell with bare stone walls. It had quite a comfortable bed, light painted walls, a chest of drawers and mats on the floor.

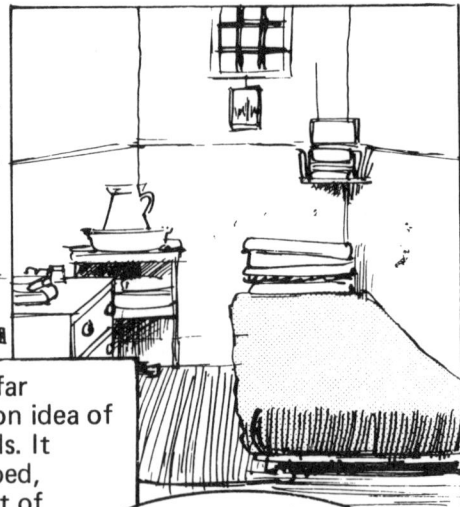

The living conditions are good but it's still a prison.

The recreation rooms in the prison had radio, T.V., table tennis, etc.

A prison visitor came to see him.

It's the monotony that gets you down.

I've heard people outside say TV and radio make prisoners soft, but comforts don't matter. It's losing your freedom that hurts.

The prisoner caused little trouble in jail and got on well with both the warders and the other prisoners.

Well, your first year's nearly up. I suppose you'll be applying for parole?

Well there's a chance anyway.

Unit 18   On parole

Vocabulary

parole	– a system where prisoners are set free before their sentence is finished; but they must behave well
serve	– (here) to stay in prison = to serve a sentence
cell	– prison room
chest of drawers	– piece of furniture, a box with drawers in it
mats	– small carpets
gets you down	– (colloquial) makes you unhappy
warders	– prison guards

Comprehension

1 How long must this man stay in prison?
2 How is his cell different from the usual idea of a cell?
3 What does he hate most about being in prison?
4 What is the prisoner going to do at the end of the first year?
5 Is he a good or a bad prisoner? How do you know?

Language work

Look at this sentence from the text:
It's the monotony that gets you down.
Many words like *get, go, take, come,* etc. change their meaning when we add *up, down, off, on, over* after the main word. Find out which words go together, and fill in the gaps in these sentences with words from the list underneath:
1 We get . . . very well together.
2 That company has taken . . . our factory.
3 He's finding it difficult to get . . . his illness.
4 I can't go . . . with you. I don't agree with that.
5 I'm afraid that doesn't come . . . to our standards.
Choose from: *on, over, up, along, off, down*

Points of view

1 What is this man's crime likely to have been? Does he seem to be a murderer, or a thief or . . .? What gives you an idea about this?
2 What makes this prison a punishment for him?
3 What does he think about the idea that radio, TV, games, etc. make prison life not too bad?
4 The prison visitor is not a friend or relative of the prisoner. Why do you think he comes to visit him?

What do you think?

1 What is the purpose of sending people to prison? What effect does it have?
2 What is the purpose of the system of parole, where prisoners can be let out early if they behave themselves? Is it a good idea? Or could it be dangerous in some cases?
3 What alternative punishments are there? Is it necessary to punish everybody who breaks the law?
4 Some prisoners are sent to prison for life, or for twenty or thirty years. What effect could this have on them? Would they stop being criminals if they were allowed to come out earlier?

Role-playing

1 Imagine you are the prisoner asking for parole. How will you persuade the authorities to let you out? What will they ask you?
2 Imagine the conversation between the prisoner and his wife, when she comes to visit him.

Written work

1 Write the prisoner's letter, asking to be let out early on parole.
2 Give your opinions about the system of law and punishment, and how it could be improved.

41

The DIVORCE COURT

Roger and Mary had been married for eight years, but the possibility of a divorce had occurred to them both for some time.

I just don't believe anything you say any longer.

In some ways it was fortunate that they had no children, although friends had other views on this.

If she'd had children things would have been different.

That's true.

In the end Roger and Mary agreed to part on friendly terms:

It's the only way. I'm sure we're being sensible.

It's a pity it didn't work out. Better see a solicitor then to see what needs to be done...

The solicitor explained the possibilities which were open to them.

I must say at the start that it is my duty to try to bring about a reconciliation between you.

If you go through with it you'll have to decide whether you want a divorce or a separation.

Then you will need to decide about the house and other financial arrangements.

Some time later:

We've decided on a divorce. We're both determined to go our own ways.

Well there is only one sure way to get a divorce these days and that is to prove that your marriage has broken down completely.

Unit 19   The divorce court

Vocabulary

divorce	– the ending of a marriage in law
had occurred to them	– they had thought about it
fortunate	– lucky, a good thing
on friendly terms	– in a friendly way
solicitor	– lawyer
reconciliation	– when people come back together after a separation
separation	– when two married people agree to live apart, but they are not legally divorced

Comprehension

1 Are the problems in Roger and Mary's marriage new ones, or have they been unhappy for some time?
2 What did they decide to do? Did they both agree?
3 Why did they see a solicitor?
4 What did he say they had to do?
5 What did the solicitor try to do first?

Points of view

1 Why didn't Mary believe anything her husband said? What does this suggest had happened in the past?
2 Why do their friends think that things would have been different if they had had children? What would have been different?
3 Why did the solicitor try to bring them back together before arranging the divorce?
4 What have they got to decide about before the divorce can be arranged?

What do you think?

1 In Britain there is one divorce for every three marriages every year. In America there is one divorce for every two marriages. What is the cause of these divorces? Were the people not suited to each other? Or have they changed?

2 Because divorce is complicated and expensive, some people say it is better not to get married at all, and therefore avoid divorce. What do you think? Should divorce be made easier?
3 If there are so many problems in marriage, why do so many people get married? What is the purpose of it in modern society? Do you think it is acceptable for people to live together without getting married?

Role-playing

1 Imagine (with another student) you are Roger and Mary, and discuss whether you should get divorced or not, giving reasons.
2 Imagine a friend of yours is having problems with his/her partner. Try to persuade them to stay together.

Written work

1 Describe the situation of marriage and divorce in your country, explaining what people think.
2 Write a letter to your parents, explaining why you and your husband/wife are going to get divorced.

Further reading

The main victims of the new wave of divorce applications seem to be not the husbands or the wives, but the second wives. It is now widely known that many people marry again after being divorced, but in some cases it can be almost financial suicide for a man to do this. If his ex-wife does not re-marry, he is obliged to pay her maintenance (money to live on) until she dies or marries again. It therefore means that some men have two families to feed, and two wives to pay for. The person who suffers is the second wife, because often the money she earns is taken to pay the first wife's maintenance!

Discussion: Describe in what circumstances this would be a fair and just law, and when it could be unjust.

INVASION of PRIVACY

Mrs. Brown answered the door:

I'm from Opinion Polls. May I ask you a few questions?

What sort of questions?

Well we're most anxious to know what you think about a number of important topics.

Do I have to answer the questions?

Well, yes. You've been selected by a computer, so it's vital I get your views. It won't take long.

Shall I come in?

Mrs. Brown let the visitor in. For twenty minutes she was asked one question after another. Some were about politics and others about advertised products.

When her husband came home:

You didn't need to answer. What a nerve!

A few weeks later Mr. Brown opened the post to find a form he had to fill in...

It's the Census. Lot of nosey questions they're asking this time.

Do you have to answer it? You told me I'd no need to with that poll.

Well this time it's different. This time the government wants to know.

Unit 20   Invasion of privacy

Vocabulary

invasion	– when someone from outside forces his way in (also used when an enemy attacks another country)
opinion poll	– finding out what people think of certain topics, to make a survey
anxious	– (here) very interested
vital	– very important
what a nerve!	– (colloquial) she had no right to do that
census	– a government count of how many people there are in the country
nosey	– (colloquial) trying to find out private information

Comprehension

1 Who was the woman at the door? What did she want?
2 What did she ask Mrs. Brown about? Did she explain what the questions were for?
3 What did Mr. Brown think about this visit? Why was he angry?
4 In what way did he feel differently when the census form came? Why?
5 How did the woman from the opinion poll persuade Mrs. Brown to answer the questions?

Points of view

1 What were the woman's motives for wanting to speak to Mrs. Brown? Why did she try and persuade her that it was so important?
2 Could there be any reasons why she wanted to talk to Mrs. Brown rather than one of the other people in that street?
3 Why did Mrs. Brown accept what the woman said, and let her into the house? Was this a dangerous thing to do?
4 What does Mr. Brown think about his privacy? What's his attitude to giving information about himself?

What do you think?

1 Who pays for this sort of opinion poll? What happens to all the information?
2 Should there be any control on opinion polls? Are they an invasion of people's privacy? Is the information they collect really necessary? How is it used?

Role-playing

Imagine you are at home and someone calls from an opinion poll. Act out the conversation, with questions and answers.

Written work

1 Describe the system in your country for making sure that your private information is not available to everybody.
2 Imagine you live in Britain and write a letter to your Member of Parliament complaining that people from opinion polls are invading your privacy.

Further reading

With the coming of computers, the amount of personal information now recorded is enormous. Each government or commercial organisation collects personal information that may be necessary for one small job. But if all that information were put together, it would give a very complete personal picture of any one individual.

This is obviously a dangerous development, and so the government must act to protect our privacy. There should be a new law giving everybody the right to find out what information about him or her is on the computer, and also correct it. People should also be able to say which information must not be passed on to other people. A Privacy Law is needed immediately.

Discussion: Do you agree with the suggestion in the text? Is this sort of law necessary? Suggest how personal information should be organised.

FIREARMS

There was l lot of controversy that summer over the question of firearms and particularly whether the police should carry guns.

The first case was one where a gang of six men armed with shotguns had robbed a bank.

They shot and killed a bank clerk and shot and wounded a bystander and a police constable.

Even so, on a TV news programme a senior police officer opposed the idea of guns for the police.

Despite all the publicity, criminals using firearms are very much in a minority.

Many people felt that if the police officer had been armed he might have stopped the gang escaping.

In the U.S.A., where the police are armed, there are over twice as many murders in a week as there are in the whole of Britain in one year.

He also said that many of these American murder victims had been shot. "But of course millions of people own guns in the U.S.A."

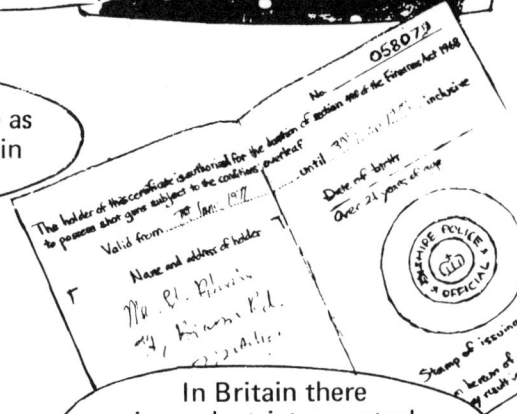

In Britain there is much stricter control over the sale and use of guns.

Almost everyone using a gun (other than a normal airgun) requires a certificate...

And children are prohibited from using guns, except in certain circumstances.

Unit 21   Firearms

Vocabulary

firearms	– weapons that use bullets – guns, rifles, etc.
controversy	– disagreement, argument
opposed	– disagreed with
requires	– needs
airgun	– simple gun for killing birds
prohibited	– not permitted by law

Comprehension

1 What was the subject of the discussion on the television news?
2 Why were people suggesting that the police should carry guns?
3 Was the police officer in favour of this idea or not?
4 What were his reasons for comparing Britain and the U.S.A.? What did he want to prove?
5 How are guns controlled in Britain?

Points of view

1 What are the views of the people who want the police to have guns? Summarise the arguments.
2 What are the views of those who disagree with giving guns to the police? Why do they disagree? (*Note:* British police never normally carry guns)
3 What are the reasons behind the system of certificates and controls for guns in Britain? What are they trying to avoid?
4 Children are not allowed to have guns. But why should they want to use them? Why do some children try and get guns to play with?

What do you think?

1 If many criminals use guns, but the police do not, how can the police control crime? Or does this situation reduce the number of criminals who use guns?
2 There are not many gun controls in America; anyone can buy a gun. Why do you think this is?
3 Why should any non-criminal people want to own a gun? What could they use it for? Should this be allowed?
4 Many children are given toy guns as presents, so they can pretend to be soldiers or cowboys. Is this safe? Or do you think it encourages violence?
5 What do you think of violence shown on television or films? Do these fantasy killings and shootings make people more or less violent?

Role-playing

1 Imagine you are the television interviewer talking to the police officer, and act out the conversation about police and guns.
2 Try and convince a friend of yours (who likes guns) that they should not be given to children as toys.

Written work

1 Describe the situation in your country. Are your police armed? Is there a lot of violence? Are most of the criminals caught and punished? Are guns carefully controlled?
2 Write to the police asking permission to have a gun. Give a good reason.

Further reading

The streets of many cities are so dangerous at night now that people must start to defend themselves. In those countries where citizens can carry guns or anti-thief sprays, one can feel a little safer, knowing that there is the possibility of frightening off some of the attackers. In America, especially, there have been great developments in weapons for self-defence, many designed especially for women. Since women are at the greatest risk, it seems only fair that Britain, too, should allow them some sort of protection against attack.

Discussion: Do you agree with the ideas here? Should people be able to defend themselves like this? Are there any dangers in legalising this sort of weapon?

SOIL EROSION

Over a period of hundreds of years farmers in many parts of the world have cleared trees, put their cattle and sheep to graze on natural grassland and ploughed up large fields to grow crops such as wheat and barley.

During hot dry summers the soil has often baked hard and cracked and crumbled.

In high winds fine soil has been blown away where trees or grassland used to keep the soil moist and held it together.

At times of heavy rainfall, channels have been formed on hill slopes...

...and much of the soil has been washed away as mud.

Farmers and scientists have worried about this problem of soil erosion. If nothing is done, the land will disappear and soil, which took thousands of years to form, will vanish completely.

One solution is to plant trees as windbreaks.

Another is to plough round a hill rather than up and down it.

Unit 22   Soil erosion

Vocabulary

soil	– the top layer of earth where plants grow
erosion	– wearing away by wind and rain
graze	– eat grass
ploughed up	– dug with long narrow lines in the ground to put seeds in
wheat	– plant whose seeds make flour and bread
barley	– plant used for food and making beer or whisky
bake	– to become very hard by the action of heat
crumble	– to break into small pieces
fine	– in very small particles
moist	– a little wet
channel	– hollowed-out course where water can flow
vanish	– go away, disappear
windbreak	– something to stop the force of the wind

Comprehension

1 What is soil erosion? Explain it simply.
2 How long has erosion been occurring?
3 What is left when the soil has been washed or blown away?
4 What is the effect of erosion on the sides of hills?
5 What does erosion mean for farmers and people living on the land?

Points of view

1 Who could be blamed for the erosion of the soil in many countries?
2 Why did many farmers want to clear trees out of their fields?
3 When the farmers cut down the trees they did it for their own benefit. What must they do now to protect their interests?
4 Is erosion a problem that governments ought to do something about, or is it for the farmers to take action?

What do you think?

1 Many parts of the world are deserts, and most deserts are getting bigger. How can we prevent this?
2 If the farmlands of the world become deserts, how else can we produce food? Or *where* else can we produce food?

Role-playing

1 Imagine you are interviewing a farmer who refuses to change his old-fashioned methods. Try and convince him of the dangers to the soil.
2 With a group of students, imagine you are a committee planning to turn a desert back into farming land. Work out how to do this.

Written work

1 Write a description of how land is used and being developed in your country.
2 Give your opinions about the way we produce food and how this may have changed one hundred years from now.

Further reading

The Sahara Desert grows in size by several hundred square kilometres each year. Land in heavily-populated countries is becoming very much over-used, and is not given enough time between crops to recover. Eventually the amount of food grown on each piece of land will be less, as the land loses its goodness. Added to that is the problem of soil erosion, which is speeded up in Britain by careless farmers who take down their hedges and trees. The result of these developments could be a world shortage of food, with millions of people dying of starvation. So what is the answer? There is obviously no single answer, but one improvement would be an increase in the amount of land reclaimed from the sea.

Discussion: What other courses of action are open to us? Is land reclamation easy in your country? Can it produce enough land to grow food for the world's population?

VANDALISM

'It has been a bad week for vandalism,' said the TV newsreader on the local 6.0.p.m. news programme — and most of the viewers agreed.

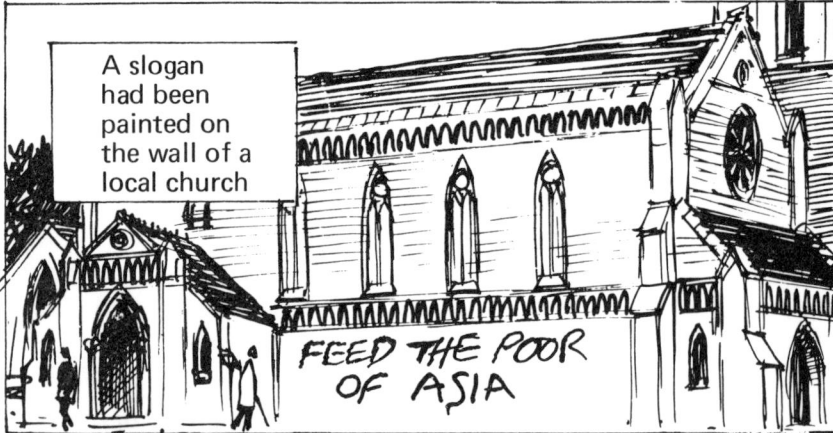

A slogan had been painted on the wall of a local church

FEED THE POOR OF ASIA

Absolutely disgraceful.

Football supporters— returning with their losing team — had broken up a railway carriage.

No more football trains from this station, that's for sure. We just can't afford it.

...while a group of apprentices kicked a football in the street and broke a shop window and dented two cars.

Two ten-year-old girls picked flowers in the town's park...

Mr. Mark Ward was not amused.

Louts! That's what they are.

Unit 23   Vandalism

Vocabulary

vandalism	– an act that destroys or damages property – bad, unlawful and usually for no reason
slogan	– a phrase or sentence often repeated, giving someone's opinion
that's for sure	– that's certain (colloquial)
apprentices	– young boys learning a skill or trade
dented	– pushed the metal in by hitting it
louts	– rough, bad-mannered men

Comprehension

1 Why did the television viewers agree with the newsreader?
2 What did the priest think about the slogan on his church?
3 What did the football fans do on the train?
4 What did the girls do wrong in the park?
5 What did Mr. Ward think of the apprentices? What were they doing?

Points of view

1 Why were people angry about the slogan on the church? Because of the message, or because it spoilt the beauty of the church?
2 If the people in the church agreed with the message, should they have been less angry about the paint on the church?
3 What were the motives for the football supporters breaking up the railway carriage? Was it only because their team had lost?
4 The apprentices broke a window by playing football – did they mean to, or might it have been an accident? Does this make it different from the actions of the football supporters?

What do you think?

1 There are several examples of damage to property here. Are they all vandalism, that is, did the people want to damage the property of others? Or are there different types of damage?
2 Which examples here would you criticise most? Why?

Role-playing

1 Imagine you are Mr. Ward. Go out and talk to the apprentices about the danger of playing football in the street. What will they say to him?
2 Make up a discussion between the priest of the church and a policeman sent to find out who painted the wall.

Written work

1 Write a letter to the football club, suggesting how they might control their supporters better.
2 Write an article on vandalism for the local paper.

Further reading

One technique that has been used very successfully recently is to make young vandals take part in community service. Instead of paying a fine (a sum of money) or even going to Borstal (the place for young criminals), they are told to spend a certain number of hours in community service. This could mean helping old people, decorating their houses, or working on some council project to make the city more beautiful. The important thing is that this sort of work seems to suggest the boys that they could use their violent energies more usefully, and many carry on the work when their 'punishment' is finished. Perhaps this shows us a way in which violence in young people could be reduced.

Discussion: Do you think this is a good way to solve the problem of young vandals? Could there be any disadvantages? How could this idea be developed with adult prisoners?

NOISE

Mary Bradley and Sarah Jones were investigating noise as part of a survey into pollution which was being carried out by their school.

Mary and Sarah made a survey of the town first but found it difficult to say how loud the noises were.

Mr. Pickering the science teacher helped.

This is what you need, Sarah.

It's a sound level meter. When you switch it on a needle tells you the sound level.

Noise is measured in decibels, but the scale used is not the same as a weight scale, for instance.

.....A reading of 110 decibels (a jet airliner taking off) is 10 times louder than a reading of 100 decibels. (The sound of a machine in a factory)

If you weigh something which is 100 kg you know it is twice as heavy as something weighing 50 kg.

110 dBA

100 dBA

90 dBA

Similarly, 90 decibels (a heavy lorry 6 metres away) is 10 times louder than 80 decibels (the back seat of my old car)

80 dBA

Unit 24   Noise

Vocabulary

investigate	– find out about something
survey	– getting facts about something and making a study of it
pollution	– dirty air, dirty water or other harmful influences on our surroundings
meter	– a machine which measures something
decibel	– a unit for measuring sound
scale	– a series of numbers to show the amounts measured, from smallest to biggest
similarly	– in the same way

Comprehension

1 Why were Mary and Sarah out in the streets of their town?
2 What did they want to measure for their survey?
3 How did their science teacher help them?
4 What is the difference between a noise at 110 decibels, and one at 100 decibels?

Points of view

1 What do the pupils hope to learn by studying pollution? Why does the school want them to know about it?
2 What makes noise pollution different from other types? Is it more or less dangerous?
3 People living in some places have serious problems with noise. What places might these be? What can be done to cut down the noise?
4 What effects can noise have on you when it is too loud? What have you noticed about it?

What do you think?

1 Some people say that we must accept a certain amount of pollution in the air or water, as well as noise, if we want a good standard of living, with factories producing many new products? What do you think? What is the opposing opinion?

2 Some pollution could be avoided; if more goods went by train instead of by lorry, the air would be cleaner. So why is this not done?

Role-playing

1 Imagine your neighbour is playing loud music at midnight. What conversation will you have?
2 You work in a factory where the noise is loud even in the office where you sit. Invent the discussion you would have with the director to try and improve the situation.

Written work

1 Write a letter to the council, complaining about the level of noise made by the workmen repairing the road outside your house. (For example, they wake you at 6 a.m.)
2 Describe your own experience of noise – what noises do you find loud, soft, unpleasant, pleasant or interesting?

Further reading

The Fairport Convention, a British rock group, gave their final concert yesterday. Their fans were very sad to think they would not hear the group again, and there were many tears at the group's farewell party after the concert. But it was inevitable. It was not that they had no more ideas, or wanted to retire. The only reason was that the leader of the group, Dave Swarbrick, was going deaf. Many years of playing in front of great piles of amplifiers at loud concerts had made him completely deaf in one ear. Now, before the second ear lost its hearing, he had to retire and live in peace and quiet. He has learned a lesson that an increasing number of musicians and concert-goers and disco-dancers are going to learn – loud music is dangerous.

Discussion: Why do many young people like music to be very loud? Is it necessary for enjoyment? How could the noise level be reduced?

RADIOACTIVITY

The atomic bombs dropped on the Japanese cities of Hiroshima and Nagasaki in 1945 killed many people years after the explosions. They died from the effects of radioactive fall-out.

In the 1950's and 1960's nuclear tests were carried out by a number of countries, including the U.K.

DAILY BRITAIN EXPLODES H-BOMB

Many people protested against the development of nuclear weapons.

EXCHESTER AND DISTRIC YOUTH CLU CND CR

ALDERMASTON MARCH LONDON

BAN U.S. OM BASES

CAMPAIGN FOR NUCLEAR DISARMAMENT

Some feared the possibility of nuclear war.

Others were worried about the effects of fall-out from these tests.

Strontium 90 can be found in milk. Large doses can be dangerous.

The radioactive dust was then analysed by scientists.

Aircraft were sent up to test the level of radioactivity in the atmosphere thousands of kilometres from the sites of the nuclear test explosions.

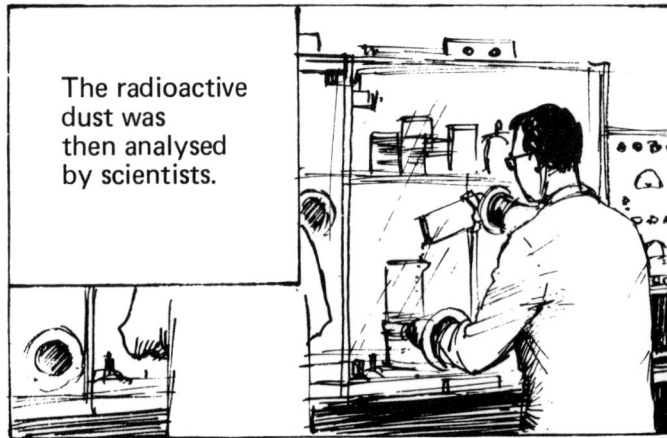

Unit 25　Radioactivity

Vocabulary

radioactivity – harmful radiation (energy) coming out of some substances; (here) in nuclear weapons

fall-out – dust with dangerous radioactive waste that fell on the earth after an atomic bomb exploded

disarmament – the act of getting rid of a country's bombs and other weapons, to reduce the possibility of war

strontium 90 – a type of radioactive material

Comprehension

1 What killed people *after* the atomic bomb exploded?
2 What did people protest about in the 1950s and 1960s?
3 What were they frightened about?
4 How could the atom bomb tests affect people's lives?
5 How did the government try to find out more about this problem?

Points of view

1 What are the views of people opposed to nuclear bombs? Explain what they are worried about.
2 Give the views of the opposing group, who feel that nuclear weapons are necessary. Which group do you belong to?
3 What makes nuclear bombs very different from ordinary bombs? What effects can this have?
4 What did the protesters against the bomb want to achieve? What did they want the government to do?

What do you think?

1 Why were nuclear weapons developed? Why did governments want them?
2 Why are so many nuclear weapons made now, even though there is no war? Is there a chance that someone might explode a nuclear bomb?
3 Nuclear energy is also used for peaceful purposes such as producing electricity. Is this a good thing to develop? Or is it as dangerous as nuclear weapons?

Role playing

Imagine you have collected a list of names of people in your town who are opposed to a plan for a nuclear power station nearby. You will be giving the list to the man who is in charge of the power station project. Work out what you will say to him.

Written work

Give your opinions on the dangers of radioactive materials, and what the world must do to make these materials safe.

Further reading

The worst fears of the anti-nuclear energy group became a reality recently with the Harrisburg, Pennsylvania disaster. Hundreds of people had to be sent out of the area because of the risk that radioactive material from the damaged power station might reach their homes. Luckily, no-one was injured or affected by radiation. But the power station was at the point where it almost began to melt down and release huge death-clouds of radiation. Some experts say that the situation was just saved in time – only a few hours more and there would have been a disaster. Surely this event gives the anti-nuclear group in Britain much more influence with the government? It's impossible to believe that anyone would want to build such a power station in Britain after what has happened; yet some stations of this type are now planned.

Discussions: Is it right to say these power stations are dangerous, after only one accident? What do you think?

WATER

The city grew and its industries flourished. But there was a snag.

The situation is serious now. It will be desperate in ten years' time.

The city was short of water.

Water Board engineers, industrialists and planners proposed many schemes. But they all centred on one beautiful area of mountains and valleys.

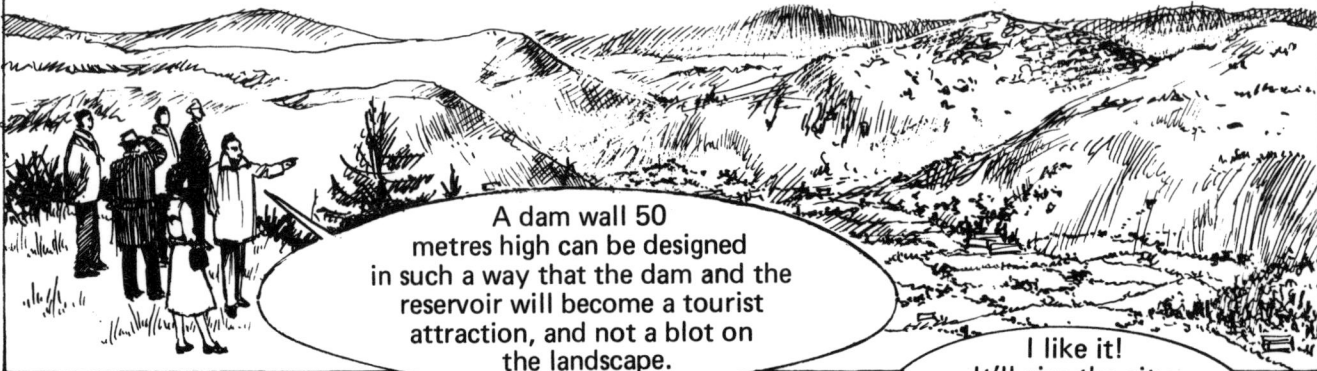

A dam wall 50 metres high can be designed in such a way that the dam and the reservoir will become a tourist attraction, and not a blot on the landscape.

I like it! It'll give the city security and it's bound to attract new industries.

What about local opinion?

We'll get round that. I don't think there'll be major opposition.

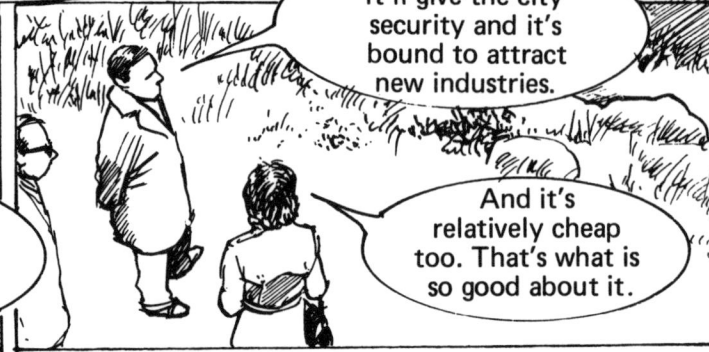

And it's relatively cheap too. That's what is so good about it.

But various groups of people did oppose the scheme and for a variety of reasons. A group of naturalists said that it might destroy several types of wildlife including birds and some rare wild flowers.

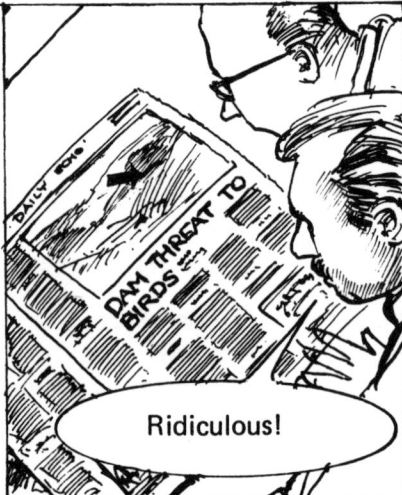

DAM THREAT TO BIRDS

Ridiculous!

SAVE THE VALLEY

Farmers, householders and tradesmen living in the valley were very angry because their land would have to be bought and they would have to move away.

Unit 26   Water

Vocabulary

flourish	– do well, become rich or successful
propose	– suggest
dam	– a wall (here: across a valley) to hold back a large amount of water
designed	– planned, arranged
reservoir	– a man-made lake or tank to store water
blot	– an ugly mark
landscape	– the shape and appearance of the countryside
security	– a feeling of being safe (here: having all the water you need)
bound to	– sure to
we'll get round that	– we'll solve that difficulty
relatively	– quite, comparatively
wildlife	– animals, birds, plants, insects, etc.
threat	– risk, possibility of harm

Comprehension

1 What was the problem which faced the city?
2 How many years were left for solving the problem?
3 What was the suggestion that the Water Board made?
4 What did they hope that people would think about their dam and reservoir?
5 How did people really feel about the plan? Which people were most angry about it?

Points of view

1 What is the city people's point of view about the dam and reservoir? Why is it so important to them?
2 We read that 'various groups' opposed the dam. What other groups are likely to protest? What sort of people might have an interest in this valley, even if they do not live in it?

What do you think?

1 Is the city justified in wanting to control the countryside like this? Which group would you support?
2 Is it really likely that the dam could become a tourist attraction? What do they mean by this?
3 What do the city planners want the water for? Is it only for drinking, or for industry also? Does this make it more important or less important?
4 What other sources of water could the city use? What about the rivers and the sea?

Role-playing

1 Imagine a public meeting to discuss this dam. You and the other students are the different groups. Give your opinions for and against the dam.
2 You are a newspaper reporter. Interview one of the farmers who would have to leave his home.

Written work

Describe the system of water supply in your own country. Does it come from rivers or dams like this one?

Further reading

Very soon we shall need a special group of water police to control how this precious resource is used. For the most annoying fact about our water is that so much of it is wasted. Too much is used in the washing of cars or watering of gardens. Toilets waste water, because they use more than is necessary each time they are flushed. If everyone put a brick inside their cistern (the water tank of the toilet) millions of gallons would be saved each year. The only answer to the water problem is to charge more money for it.

Discussion: Do you agree that water is wasted? Should we charge a lot for it? Would this make people use less?

World Resources

In 1952 huge iron ore deposits were discovered by chance in North-West Australia when the plane carrying an Australian cattle rancher had to change course because of cloud. The plane flew between the sides of a gorge which appeared to be made of iron.

Today the iron ore deposits of the Hamersley mountains form one of the largest iron ore fields in the world.

Iron ore nowadays is Australia's most important mineral export.

Over a hundred years ago other miners could be seen in Australia.

These were the gold miners and many thriving towns grew up in the gold mining areas.

Today many of these old mining towns are ghost towns.

Once the gold ore had been mined out, the miners left and many buildings fell into ruins.

Unit 27 World resources

Vocabulary

resources   – supplies of materials (here: our natural substances)

gorge   – narrow valley with steep sides

iron ore deposits   – places where iron in un-refined form is found in the ground

rancher   – man who owns land on which he keeps cattle

change course– change direction, go another way

mineral   – natural material, e.g. stone, iron, coal, diamonds, found in the earth

thriving   – doing well, successful

ghost town   – town which is now empty; the people have left but the buildings are still there

Comprehension

1 What was discovered in Australia? In which region was it?
2 How was the deposit discovered? Were the people looking for it?
3 Why is iron ore so important to Australia?
4 What else was mined in Australia?
5 What happened to the mining towns that were once so busy?

Points of view

1 Iron ore brings a lot of money into Australia, so it is mined quickly and in great quantity. What is the danger here? What will happen in a hundred years?
2 How could iron ore resources be used in a better way?
3 What will happen when there is no more iron ore? What will the miners and the ore companies do then?
4 Does the uncertain future of iron ore mining have any similarities with the future of another natural resource that the world uses?

What do you think?

1 Who controls most world resources? Is it the poor countries who have the minerals etc, or the rich countries who buy these things? Where might conflict occur?
2 One of the biggest problems is energy – where do you think we shall get our energy in a hundred years' time?
3 Certain materials (such as aluminium) may soon run out completely. What effect will this have on our lives?
4 Is there anything that people as individuals can do to make world resources last longer?

Role-playing

1 Imagine you are the boss of an iron ore mining company. You know that your iron ore will run out in five years. What can you do? Discuss it with your colleagues.
2 Work out with other students how society must change in order to save resources for the future. Make a plan.

Written work

Suggest how resources can be saved and what changes are needed in our life-style.

Further reading

Building new power stations isn't going to solve the basic problems of energy. What we need to do is to think about alternatives – alternative ways of living, and therefore alternative ways of making energy. There is a lot of power in the seas and the winds and in the heat of the sun. But to use it we must think more carefully about our needs for energy. Too much of it is wasted on unnecessary machines such as electric knives and electric egg boilers that do work which we could do ourselves just as well. We must get rid of such things and get back to a simpler way of life before we can solve the energy problem.

Discussion: Do you agree that we waste energy? Give some examples.

ENTERPRISE ⚓ NEPTUNE

In 1965 the National Trust launched a campaign to help save the coastline of parts of Britain. Their initial target then was £2 million and the success of the project was shown by the fact that by 1973 they had acquired over 300 kilometres of coastline for the nation.

An official explains:

The problem we face is that each year more and more people spend holidays at the coast.

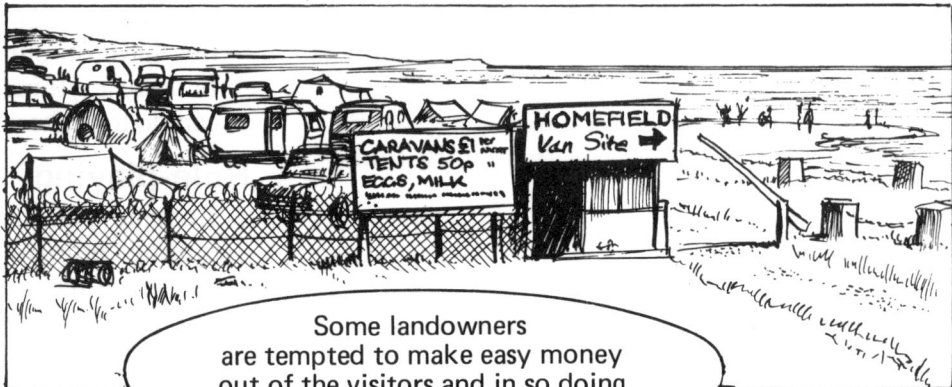

Some landowners are tempted to make easy money out of the visitors and in so doing they spoil the coastline.

Caravan sites are sometimes allowed to develop on beautiful areas by the sea shore, instead of being hidden from view.

Nobody wants to stop holidaymakers in cars and caravans, but if something isn't done soon to control things there won't be any unspoilt coastline by the end of the century.

Unit 28   Enterprise Neptune

Vocabulary

The National Trust	– an organisation that protects beautiful parts of Britain and looks after historic buildings
target	– something to aim at.
launch	– (here) start (usually: send a ship on its first trip)
campaign	– an organised plan with a special purpose
initial	– at the beginning
acquired	– got, obtained (here: bought)
official	– someone who has a job with an organisation (here: works for the National Trust)
tempt	– make someone want to do something
caravan sites	– special parks for holiday caravans
shore	– where the sea meets the land
century	– one hundred years

Comprehension

1 Why did the National Trust start a big campaign?
2 What did they do with the money they received?
3 Who spoils the coastline? Why do they do this? What advantages are there for them?
4 Where should the caravan sites be?
5 What will happen if caravan sites are not controlled?

Points of view

1 Why is the National Trust buying land (and buildings) around Britain? Why does it think it necessary to take control of these things?
2 Why is the Trust unhappy about caravan sites, which provide cheap holidays for many people?
3 What about the people who use these places? What do they think of the caravan sites and the coastline?
4 What do local shopkeepers think?

What do you think?

1 In what sort of place would you like to spend your holiday – an empty and unspoilt area, or one with plenty of entertainments?
2 What do you think the majority of people prefer?
3 Is it possible to prevent the development of a holiday area? Is it fair to stop new hotels or caravan sites? What are the arguments for and against control?

Role-playing

Imagine the discussion between a farmer who wants to sell his land to a hotel company, and the National Trust official who wants to buy it.

Written work

Describe a holiday area that you know well, and explain how you would like to protect it for the future.

Further reading

The values of tourism as a means of communication have often been described. People of different nationalities get together and forget nationalistic stereotypes. They learn each other's language and customs, and develop a much more tolerant view of each other. In the long run this helps to prevent wars, because people are less likely to want to fight each other. The problem is that so often this idea doesn't work in practice. When people go abroad, they hate the food and the high prices, they feel the waiters are cheating them, they wish they were back at home. If they do talk to foreigners, they are likely to have arguments about football, politics or which country has the best weather. Added to this, tourists are dirty and untidy. They bring commercial ideas to quiet unspoilt areas, and so make themselves more unpopular.

Discussion: Do you agree that tourists do not give a good image of their country? What do you think of tourists in your country?

Discussion phrases

These are the most common ways in English of joining in with a discussion, and students should practise as many as possible in their discussion work.

Expressing an opinion

I think that . . .
I believe that . . .
Personally, I feel . . .
The point is that . . .
In my opinion . . .
I'd like to say that . . .

Asking for someone's opinion

What do you think about . . .?
How do you feel about . . .?
What's your opinion of . . .?
What would you say about . . .?

Agreeing with someone

That's true.
That's right.
That's a good point.
I agree entirely.
I agree completely.
You're absolutely right.

Disagreeing with someone

That's not the point.
That's not (entirely) true.
I'm afraid I disagree.
Surely the *real* point is . . .
I can't agree with that . . .